Natalie Gomez

Beverly Cleary
She Makes Reading Fun

Patricia Stone Martin

illustrated by Karen Park

Rourke Enterprises Vero Beach, Florida

Manufactured in the United States of America

Library of Congress Cataloging-in-Publication Data

Martin, Patricia Stone.
    Beverly Cleary – she makes reading fun.

    (Reaching your goal biographies)
    Summary: A brief biography of the popular author,
focusing on how she became a writer. Includes
information on setting goals.
    1. Cleary, Beverly – Biography – Juvenile literature.
2. Authors, American – 20th century – Biography –
Juvenile literature. 3. Children's literature – Authorship –
Juvenile literature. [1. Cleary, Beverly. 2. Authors,
American. 3. Authorship] I. Title. II. Series:
Martin, Patricia Stone. Reaching your goal biographies.
PS3553.L3914Z78 1987 813'.54 [B] 87-12122
ISBN 0-86592-171-7

Beverly Bunn sat in the row closest to the blackboard. She was with her first-grade reading group. The teacher held up cards. "Sip, sit, red, rill, bib, bed," read Beverly slowly. It was very hard. She looked at the children by the window. They did not think reading was hard. Beverly looked at the word cards again. There must be a secret to reading, she thought. Reading is no fun.

Beverly worked hard to learn to read. She worked hard in second grade too. Then one day in third grade, something wonderful happened. Beverly found a book that she liked. She tried to read it, and she did! She read all the rest of that day. Suddenly reading was fun.

Beverly read from that day on. She read every book she could find. Many of the books came from the library. The librarian got to know Beverly quite well! She said that Beverly should write books for children.

Beverly liked that idea. When she grew up, she decided, she would write books for children. The children in the books would be like herself. The books would be fun to read.

That's exactly what Beverly did. You have probably read books by Beverly Bunn Cleary.

Beverly Cleary was born on April 12, 1916, in McMinnville, Oregon. She grew up in a big old house. The house was on a beautiful farm near Yamhill. Beverly played alone on the farm and was very happy.

Yamhill was too small to have a library. Mrs. Bunn set up a library in Yamhill. She had books sent from a larger town nearby. Beverly loved seeing all of the books. She liked the children's books best. She wished she could read them by herself.

When Beverly was six, her family moved to Portland. Portland was a city, and Beverly was excited. She would make new friends. She could go to a big library with lots of books. She would learn to read all of them.

But reading was not easy for Beverly. There were three reading groups in her first grade. The Bluebirds were the good readers. The Redbirds were the middle readers. And the Blackbirds were the slow readers. Beverly was a Blackbird.

Second grade was better. She could read some stories. But she did not want to read. The stories were no fun.

But in third grade, everything changed. She found some stories that she liked. She became a good reader!

Beverly knew she wanted to be a writer when she grew up. Her mother said she should get a job first. So Beverly studied to be a children's librarian. Part of her job was to hold story hours on Saturdays. She always chose fun stories to read aloud.

In 1940, Beverly married Clarence T. Cleary. They moved to Oakland, California. World War II began the next year. Beverly became a librarian at the Oakland Army Hospital during the war.

After the war, the Clearys bought a house in Berkeley, California, not far from Oakland. Beverly found some typing paper in one of the closets. She told her husband she would have to write a book. Why didn't she? he asked. Because she never had a sharpened pencil, she answered. The next day, Mr. Cleary brought home a pencil sharpener!

Beverly worked in a bookstore that Christmas. She sold children's books. She read many of the books. "I can write better stories than some of these," she said.

After Christmas she began to write. She wrote about a little boy who found a stray dog. He could keep the dog if he could get it home on a bus. Many funny things happened. The little boy was Henry Huggins. His dog was Ribsy.

Beverly wrote five or six books before she had any children. Then the Clearys had twins, a boy and a girl. They named the twins Marianne Elisabeth and Malcolm James.

Beverly kept writing books. Many of the children in her books have become well known to readers. Henry Huggins, Ramona and Beezus Quimby, Ellen Tebbits, and Runaway Ralph are some of their favorites. Beverly's son wanted a story about a motorcycle. She wrote *The Mouse and the Motorcycle* to please him. The story is about a hotel mouse who can ride a toy motorcycle.

Most of Beverly Cleary's books are about everyday things that happen to children. She wants children to see themselves in her books. Most of all, she wants her books to be funny.

And her books *are* funny. In *Ramona Quimby, Age 8*, this happens: Ramona takes a hard-boiled egg to school for lunch. The big thing at school is to crack your egg open by hitting it on your head. All morning long, Ramona looks forward to cracking her egg. At lunch, she makes sure everyone is watching. Then she whacks the egg against her head. Ramona's mother has forgotten to cook the egg!

Beverly Cleary has won many awards for her books. Her biggest reward is knowing that children like to read her books. She is still writing books. Some of her stories are even going to be on television. Beverly Cleary has reached her goal. She has written books that are fun to read.

Reaching Your Goal

What are your goals? Here are some steps to help you reach them.

1. Decide on your goal.
   It may be a short-term goal like one of these:
   learning to ride a bike
   getting a good grade on a test
   keeping your room clean
   It may be a long-term goal like one of these:
   learning to read
   learning to play the piano
   becoming a lawyer

2. Decide if your goal is something you really can do.
   Do you have the talent you need?
   How can you find out? By trying!
   Will you need special equipment?
   Perhaps you need a piano or ice skates.
   How can you get what you need?
   Ask your teacher or your parents.

3. Decide on the first thing you must do.
Perhaps this will be to take lessons.

4. Decide on the second thing you must do.
Perhaps this will be to practice every day.

5. Start right away.
Stick to your plan until you reach your goal.

6. Keep telling yourself, "I can do it!"

Good luck! Maybe someday you will become a famous writer like Beverly Cleary.

Reaching Your Goal Books

Beverly Cleary
She Makes Reading Fun

Bill Cosby Superstar

Jesse Jackson A Rainbow Leader

Ted Kennedy, Jr.
A Lifetime of Challenges

Christa McAuliffe
Reaching for the Stars

Dale Murphy
Baseball's Gentle Giant

Dr. Seuss We Love You

Samantha Smith Young Ambassador

Rourke Enterprises, Inc.
P.O. Box 3328
Vero Beach, FL 32964